I0815355

The Titanic
Sinking & Rescue

by Julie Murray

Level 1 – Beginning
Short and simple sentences with familiar words or patterns for children who are beginning to understand how letters and sounds go together.

Level 2 – Emerging
Longer words and sentences with more complex language patterns for readers who are practicing common words and letter sounds.

Level 3 – Transitional
More developed language and vocabulary for readers who are becoming more independent.

abdobooks.com

Published by Abdo Zoom, a division of ABDO, PO Box 398166, Minneapolis, Minnesota 55439.

Printed in the United States of America, North Mankato, Minnesota.
102024
012025

Photo Credits: Getty Images, Granger Collection, Shutterstock
Production Contributors: Kenny Abdo, Jennie Forsberg, Grace Hansen, John Hansen
Design Contributors: Candice Keimig, Neil Klinepier

Library of Congress Control Number: 2024936547

Publisher's Cataloging in Publication Data

Names: Murray, Julie, author.
Title: The Titanic sinking & rescue / by Julie Murray
Description: Minneapolis, Minnesota : Abdo Zoom, 2025 | Series: History of the Titanic | Includes online resources and index.
Identifiers: ISBN 9781098287276 (lib. bdg.) | ISBN 9781098287979 (ebook) | ISBN 9781098288327 (Read-to-me ebook)
Subjects: LCSH: Shipwrecks--North Atlantic Ocean--Juvenile literature. | Search and rescue operations--Juvenile literature. | Historic ships--Juvenile literature. | Shipwreck survival--Juvenile literature. | Titanic (Steamship)--Juvenile literature.
Classification: DDC 910.9163--dc23

Table of Contents

Sinking & Rescue of the Titanic
4

On April 14, 1912, at 11:40 p.m. the **RMS** *Titanic* hit an **iceberg**. It resulted in one of the worst disasters in history at sea.

The **iceberg** split the ship's **hull** open. Water rushed in. The compartment doors couldn't stop the flooding.

The ship's alarms went off. Passengers came up to the deck. No one could have guessed that the "unsinkable" ship was in trouble.

The *Titanic* had just enough lifeboats for half of the people onboard. Women and children were told to get on the lifeboats first.

The front of the ship went down first. Then it broke in half. At 2:20 a.m. on April 15, 1912, the *Titanic* sank.

1.50 AM.
RD END FLOATS, THEN SINKS
2.00 AM.
STERN SECTION PIVOTS AMIDSHIPS AND SWINGS OVER SPOT WHERE FORWARD SECTION SANK.
LAST Position In which "Titanic" stayed 5 minutes Before the FINAL plunge.
L.P. Skidmore.
S.S. "Carpathia". Apr. 15th 1912.

The ocean water was 28° F (-2° C). Many people died from **hypothermia**.

To the Rescue

Before the *Titanic* sank, operators sent out distress calls. They hoped another ship was in the area.

The **RMS** *Carpathia* was 58 miles (93 km) away. It raced toward the *Titanic*. It arrived around 3:30 a.m.

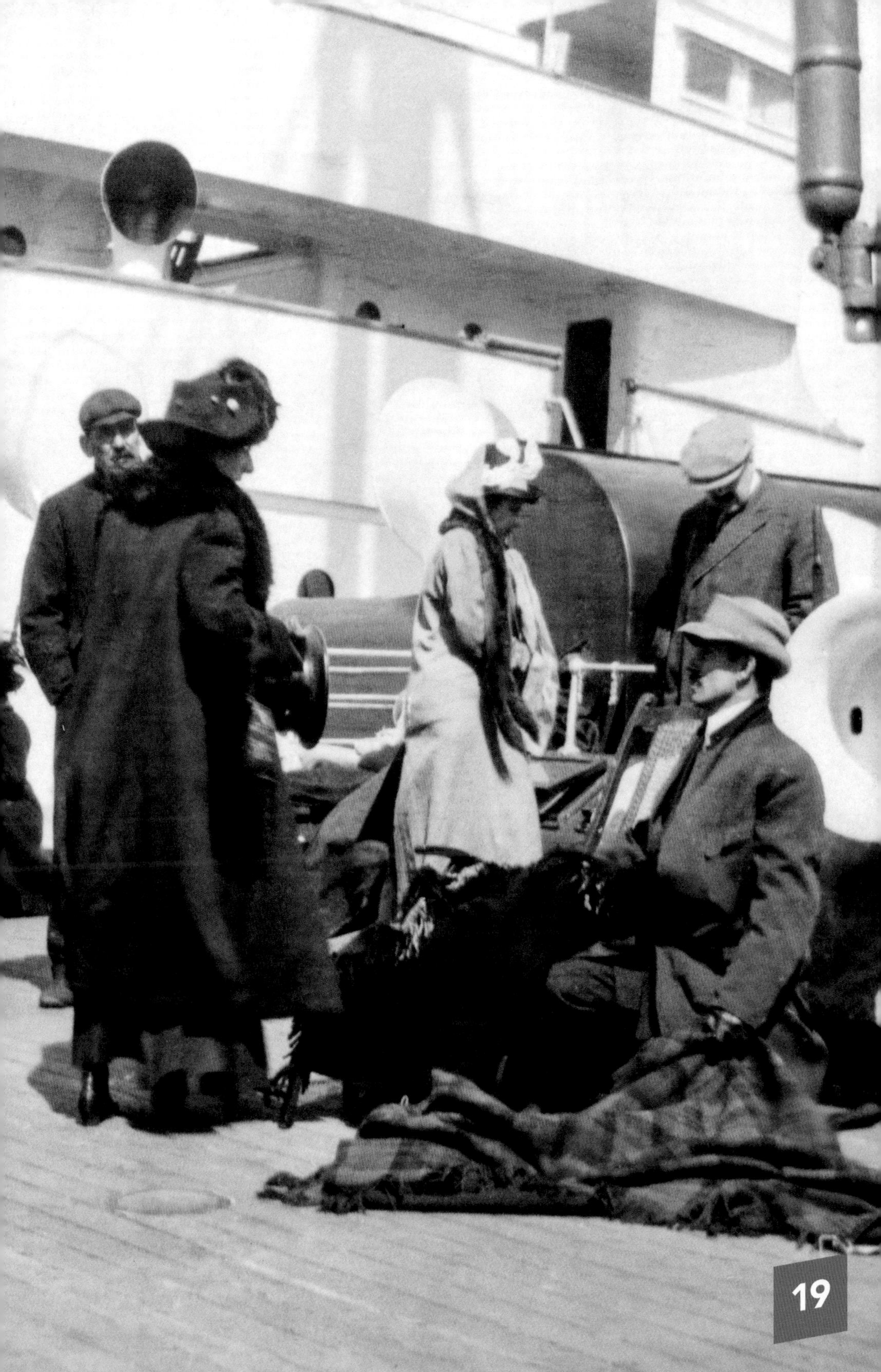

TITANIC
DISASTER
GREAT LOSS
OF LIFE
EVENING NEWS

The *Carpathia* picked up 705 people in lifeboats. It headed toward New York City, the *Titanic's* destination. The ship arrived there on April 18, 1912.

More Facts

- The *Titanic* was moving 23.6 miles per hour (38 kph) when it hit the **iceberg**.
- An eight-member band played music as the ship sank.
- More than 1,500 people lost their lives in the sinking of the *Titanic*.

Glossary

hull - the rigid frame and outer shell of a ship.

hypothermia - a condition of very low body temperature.

iceberg - a large floating mass of ice that has broken from a glacier.

RMS - short for Royal Mail Ship.

Index

Online Resources

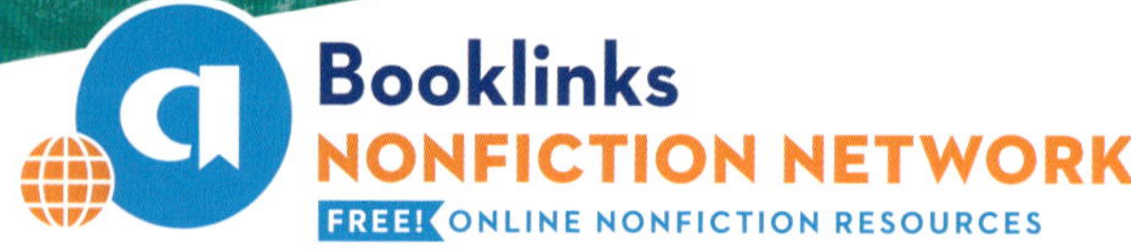

To learn more about the sinking & rescue of the *Titanic*, please visit **abdobooklinks.com** or scan this QR code. These links are routinely monitored and updated to provide the most current information available.